DK findout!
Sharks

Author and consultant: Sarah Fowler, OBE

Editor Olivia Stanford
Senior art editor Katie Knutton
Design assistant Rhea Gaughan
Jacket co-ordinator Francesca Young
Jacket designer Amy Keast
Managing editor Laura Gilbert
Managing art editor Diane Peyton Jones
Pre-production producer Dragana Puvacic
Producer Srijana Gurung
Art director Martin Wilson
Publisher Sarah Larter
Publishing director Sophie Mitchell

Educational consultant Jacqueline Harris

First published in Great Britain in 2017 by
Dorling Kindersley Limited
80 Strand, London, WC2R 0RL

Copyright © 2017 Dorling Kindersley Limited
A Penguin Random House Company
10 9 8 7 6 5 4 3 2 1
001–298644–Jan/2017

A CIP catalogue record for this book
is available from the British Library.
ISBN: 978-0-2412-8273-1

Printed and bound in China

A WORLD OF IDEAS:
SEE ALL THERE IS TO KNOW

www.dk.com

Contents

The scale boxes
throughout the book
show you how big a shark
is compared to a diver
who is 1.8 m (6 ft) tall
from head to heel.

»Scale

Great white shark

2

Prickly dogfish

Great hammerhead

Whale shark

Horn shark

Frilled shark

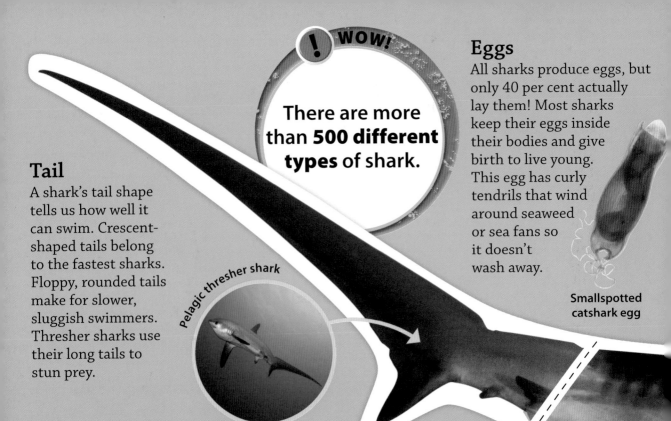

! WOW!

There are more than **500 different types** of shark.

Tail

A shark's tail shape tells us how well it can swim. Crescent-shaped tails belong to the fastest sharks. Floppy, rounded tails make for slower, sluggish swimmers. Thresher sharks use their long tails to stun prey.

Pelagic thresher shark

Eggs

All sharks produce eggs, but only 40 per cent actually lay them! Most sharks keep their eggs inside their bodies and give birth to live young. This egg has curly tendrils that wind around seaweed or sea fans so it doesn't wash away.

Smallspotted catshark egg

What is a shark?

Sharks are fish, but unlike most other kinds of fish they have a flexible skeleton made of a material called cartilage instead of bone. They have gills behind their head to breathe and their strong tail powers them forwards. Two pectoral fins keep them stable in the water as they swim around searching for food to eat. All sharks are meat-eaters!

Tiger shark

Body

A shark's muscles are attached to the inside of its skin. Outside, the skin is armoured with tiny plates, called denticles, that streamline the body. Many sharks have colourful or patterned skin, such as the tiger shark.

Dorsal fin

Blacktip reef shark

Most sharks have two dorsal fins on their back. These fins help to stabilise a shark when it swims. Their shape and colour can be used to identify the type of shark – it's easy to spot a blacktip reef shark!

Head

Many of a shark's sense organs are found on its head. As well as the eyes, ears, and nose, it has special organs that detect electricity. Hammerheads have more of these organs than any other shark.

Scalloped hammerhead

Pectoral fins

Australian angelshark

Like flaps on an aeroplane wing, the pectoral fins on a shark's sides help to steer it and prevent it from rolling over! Sharks that live on the seabed, such as angelsharks, also use their strong pectorals for swimming or walking.

How big?

Not many people realize, but big sharks are fairly unusual. Most shark species are less than 1 m (3 ft) long, and the tiniest of all are under 30 cm (12 in). Large sharks hunt big prey, however, the most enormous sharks of all are filter feeders. They eat tiny sea creatures called plankton. Plankton may be small, but filter feeders eat a lot of it!

Basking shark

The world's second-biggest fish can grow up to 10 m (33 ft) long. The basking shark often swims near the surface, which is where it gets its name. However, it isn't warming itself in the sun, but feeding on plankton there.

Tiny sharks

Some adult sharks are so small they could fit into your hand! The biggest pygmy shark ever seen was 27 cm (11 in) long. Their young are really tiny, only 6–10 cm (2–4 in) long. Each mum has eight baby sharks.

! WOW!

Many adult sharks grow less than **1 cm (0.4 in)** a year, taking **decades** to reach full size!

These sharks are compared in size to an adult human measuring 1.8 m (6 ft) tall.

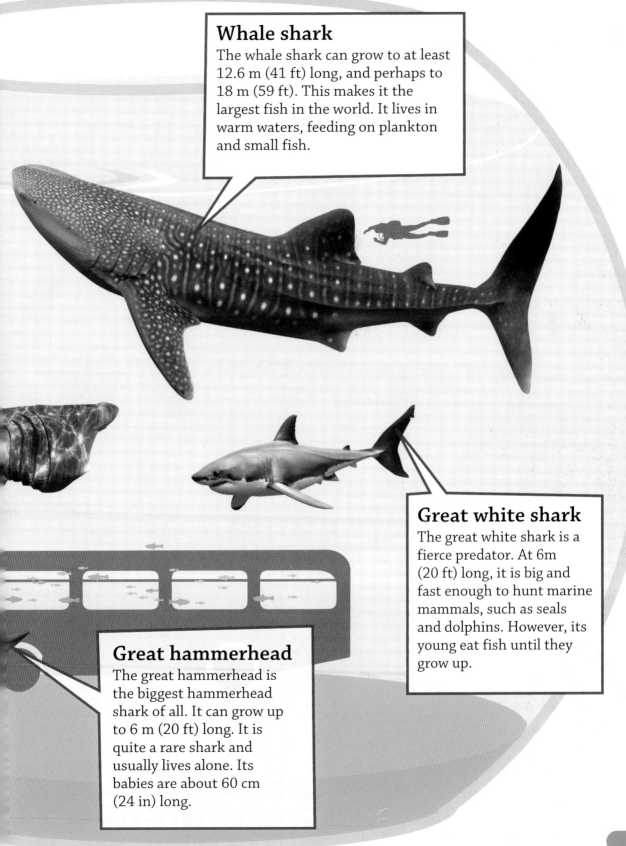

Whale shark

The whale shark can grow to at least 12.6 m (41 ft) long, and perhaps to 18 m (59 ft). This makes it the largest fish in the world. It lives in warm waters, feeding on plankton and small fish.

Great white shark

The great white shark is a fierce predator. At 6m (20 ft) long, it is big and fast enough to hunt marine mammals, such as seals and dolphins. However, its young eat fish until they grow up.

Great hammerhead

The great hammerhead is the biggest hammerhead shark of all. It can grow up to 6 m (20 ft) long. It is quite a rare shark and usually lives alone. Its babies are about 60 cm (24 in) long.

Prehistoric sharks

The oldest whole-shark fossil is about 409 million years old – that's almost 200 million years older than the first dinosaurs! A shark's soft skeleton doesn't fossilize easily, but their teeth, fin spines, and scales are almost indestructible. These provide many clues about the peculiar, prehistoric sharks below.

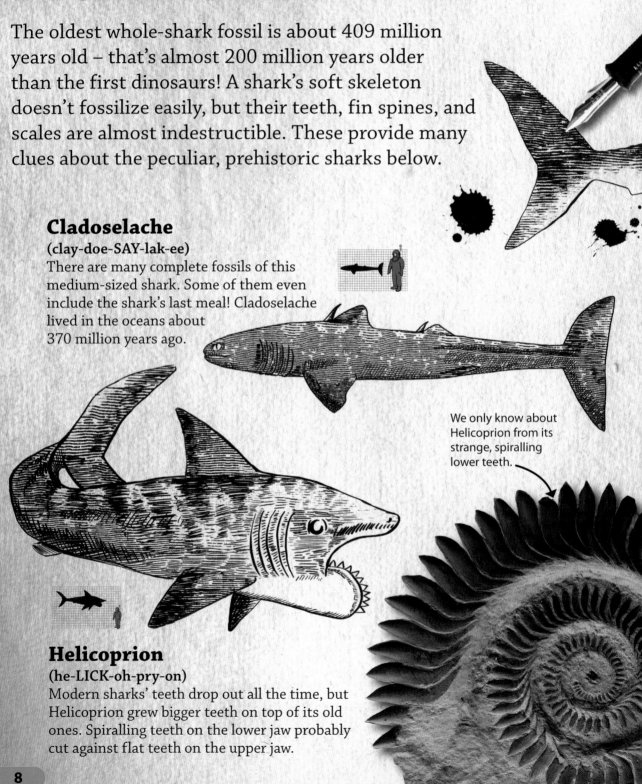

Cladoselache
(clay-doe-SAY-lak-ee)
There are many complete fossils of this medium-sized shark. Some of them even include the shark's last meal! Cladoselache lived in the oceans about 370 million years ago.

We only know about Helicoprion from its strange, spiralling lower teeth.

Helicoprion
(he-LICK-oh-pry-on)
Modern sharks' teeth drop out all the time, but Helicoprion grew bigger teeth on top of its old ones. Spiralling teeth on the lower jaw probably cut against flat teeth on the upper jaw.

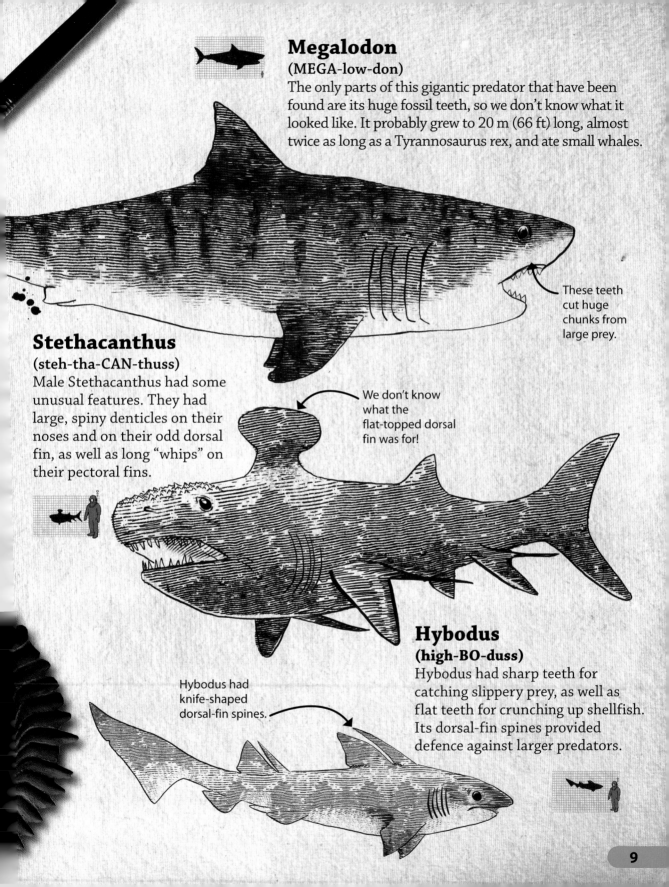

Megalodon
(MEGA-low-don)
The only parts of this gigantic predator that have been found are its huge fossil teeth, so we don't know what it looked like. It probably grew to 20 m (66 ft) long, almost twice as long as a Tyrannosaurus rex, and ate small whales.

These teeth cut huge chunks from large prey.

Stethacanthus
(steh-tha-CAN-thuss)
Male Stethacanthus had some unusual features. They had large, spiny denticles on their noses and on their odd dorsal fin, as well as long "whips" on their pectoral fins.

We don't know what the flat-topped dorsal fin was for!

Hybodus
(high-BO-duss)
Hybodus had sharp teeth for catching slippery prey, as well as flat teeth for crunching up shellfish. Its dorsal-fin spines provided defence against larger predators.

Hybodus had knife-shaped dorsal-fin spines.

Shark relatives

Sharks aren't the only fish with skeletons made of cartilage. They have many close relatives: the rays, including skates and sawfish, and chimaeras. A few rays look rather shark-like, such as the saw-nosed sawfish, but most appear quite different, with flat bodies and "wings".

ELECTRIC RAYS

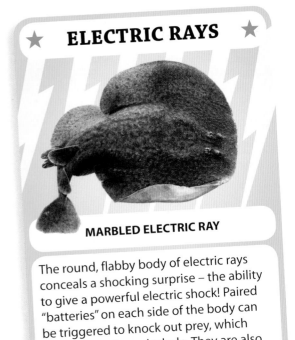

MARBLED ELECTRIC RAY

The round, flabby body of electric rays conceals a shocking surprise – the ability to give a powerful electric shock! Paired "batteries" on each side of the body can be triggered to knock out prey, which are then swallowed whole. They are also used to stun predators.

STINGRAYS

SPOTTED EAGLE RAY

Stingrays have a whip-like tail that may have one or two stinging spines, used for defence. They give birth to live pups rather than laying eggs. Eagle rays are a type of stingray that live in tropical waters and eat shellfish.

CHIMAERAS

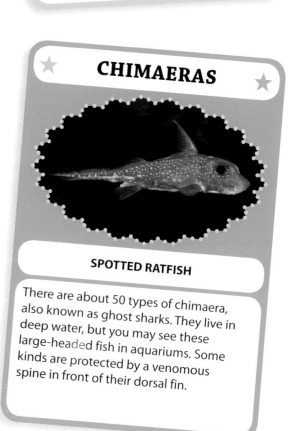

SPOTTED RATFISH

There are about 50 types of chimaera, also known as ghost sharks. They live in deep water, but you may see these large-headed fish in aquariums. Some kinds are protected by a venomous spine in front of their dorsal fin.

GUITARFISH ⭐

ATLANTIC GUITARFISH

These rays have a triangular head and a strong, shark-like tail, which gives them a guitar-shaped outline when seen from above. They use their pointed noses to dig for prey buried beneath the sand. There are around 50 species of guitarfish.

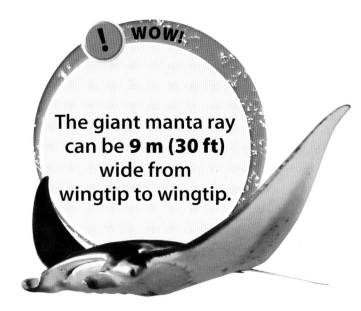

! WOW!

The giant manta ray can be **9 m (30 ft)** wide from wingtip to wingtip.

SKATES

THORNBACK SKATE

There are over 200 kinds of skate. They have fatter tails than rays, and instead of stinging spines, they have tiny dorsal fins near the end. They lay each of their eggs in a case, which may be found washed up on a beach after the baby fish has hatched.

⭐ SAWFISH ⭐

LARGETOOTH SAWFISH

Shaped like a flat shark, but with their gills hidden under their heads, these warm-water coastal rays are extremely rare and often strictly protected. Unfortunately, their toothed noses, called rostra, still turn up in curiosity shops.

Shark detective

Sharks don't all look the same. Scientists use sharks' physical features to divide them into different groups. In total there are nine groups, or orders, of shark. Answer these questions to sort any type of shark into its correct order.

Bramble sharks

Go to page 18 to bump into these prickly, deepwater sharks.

Prickly shark

YES

Does it have two small dorsal fins and thorny skin?

NO | **NO**

START HERE

Does it have more than five gill slits and only one dorsal fin on its back?

NO

Does it have a small fin near the base of its tail?

YES

Does it have spines on its dorsal fins?

NO

YES

Spine on dorsal fin

Cow and frilled sharks

Go to page 14 to learn about the world's most ancient sharks.

Seven gill slits

Broadnose sevengill shark

Bullhead sharks

Go to page 20 to learn more about the sharks with eyebrows.

Port Jackson shark

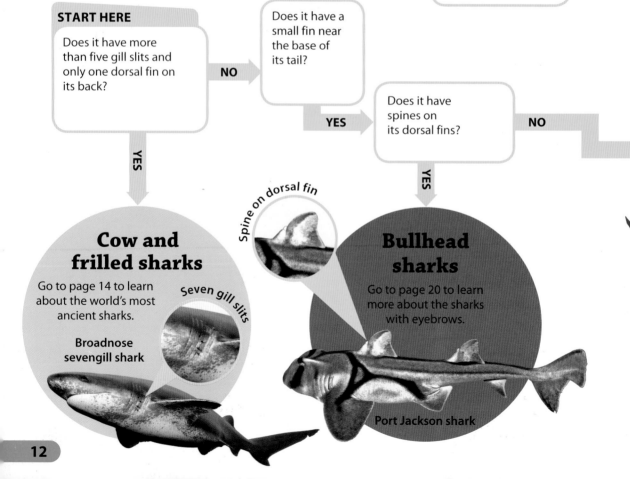

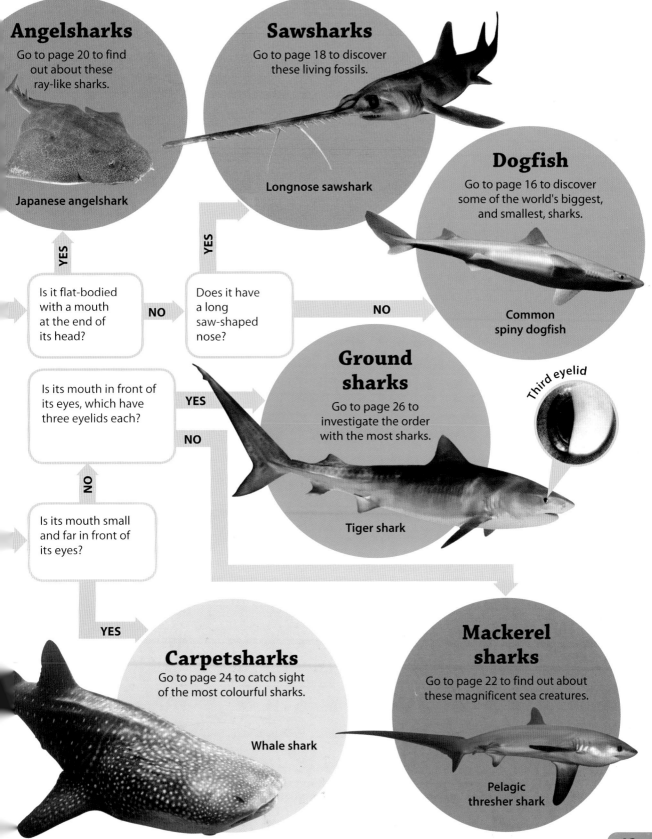

Angelsharks

Go to page 20 to find out about these ray-like sharks.

Japanese angelshark

Sawsharks

Go to page 18 to discover these living fossils.

Longnose sawshark

Dogfish

Go to page 16 to discover some of the world's biggest, and smallest, sharks.

Common spiny dogfish

YES

YES

Is it flat-bodied with a mouth at the end of its head?

NO

Does it have a long saw-shaped nose?

NO

Is its mouth in front of its eyes, which have three eyelids each?

YES

NO

Ground sharks

Go to page 26 to investigate the order with the most sharks.

Tiger shark

Third eyelid

NO

Is its mouth small and far in front of its eyes?

YES

Carpetsharks

Go to page 24 to catch sight of the most colourful sharks.

Whale shark

Mackerel sharks

Go to page 22 to find out about these magnificent sea creatures.

Pelagic thresher shark

Frilled shark

This mysterious, brown, eel-like shark lives in the deep sea and is rarely seen. However, the frilled shark is instantly recognizable because of its snake-like head and large mouth filled with needle-sharp teeth.

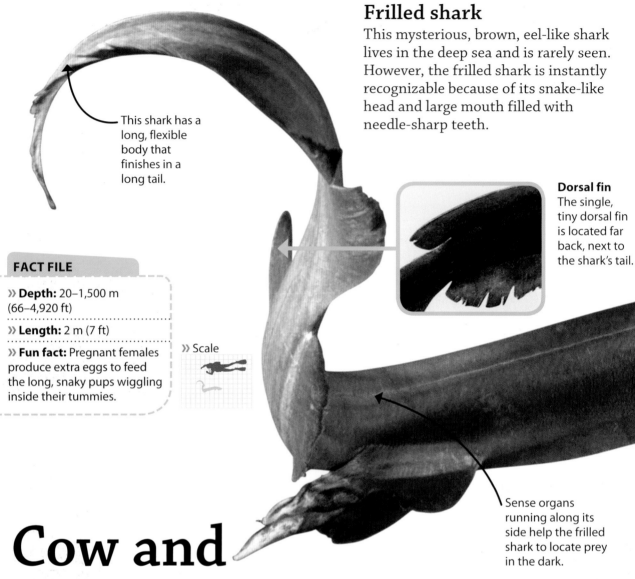

This shark has a long, flexible body that finishes in a long tail.

Dorsal fin
The single, tiny dorsal fin is located far back, next to the shark's tail.

FACT FILE

» **Depth:** 20–1,500 m (66–4,920 ft)

» **Length:** 2 m (7 ft)

» **Fun fact:** Pregnant females produce extra eggs to feed the long, snaky pups wiggling inside their tummies.

» Scale

Sense organs running along its side help the frilled shark to locate prey in the dark.

Cow and frilled sharks

These two families of fish make up the oldest, most primitive order of sharks. There are only two frilled shark species and four cow shark species. They all have six or seven gill slits instead of the usual five, and only one dorsal fin. These sharks like cold water and most live in the deep ocean, but sometimes they journey into cool coastal seas.

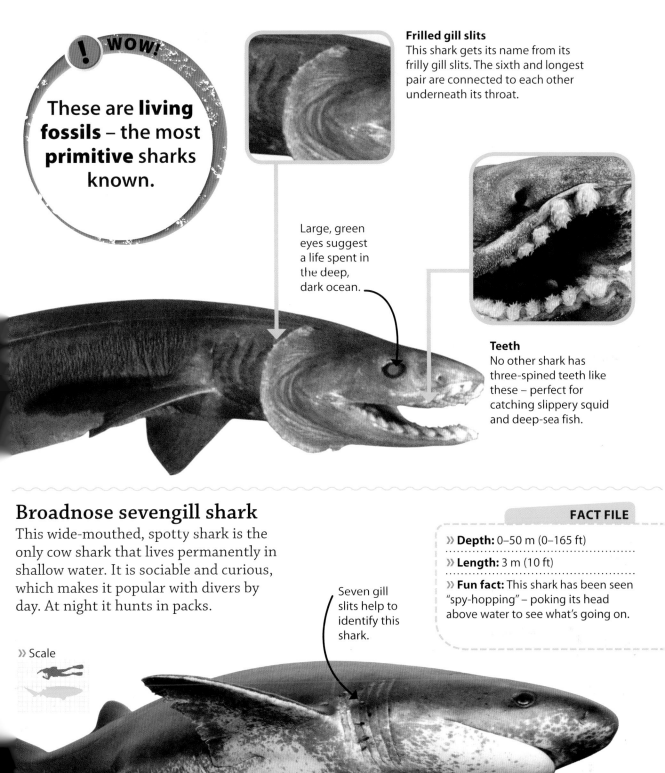

Frilled gill slits
This shark gets its name from its frilly gill slits. The sixth and longest pair are connected to each other underneath its throat.

Large, green eyes suggest a life spent in the deep, dark ocean.

Teeth
No other shark has three-spined teeth like these – perfect for catching slippery squid and deep-sea fish.

Broadnose sevengill shark

This wide-mouthed, spotty shark is the only cow shark that lives permanently in shallow water. It is sociable and curious, which makes it popular with divers by day. At night it hunts in packs.

Seven gill slits help to identify this shark.

» Scale

FACT FILE

» **Depth:** 0–50 m (0–165 ft)

» **Length:** 3 m (10 ft)

» **Fun fact:** This shark has been seen "spy-hopping" – poking its head above water to see what's going on.

Dogfish

The 130 kinds of dogfish sharks are scattered throughout the world's oceans. Some live in shallow seas or estuaries, where rivers run into the sea. Others live in the deep ocean. This group includes the only sharks that live under polar ice sheets, but many more can only survive in the warm tropics.

Common spiny dogfish

This widespread dogfish used to be the most common shark in the North Atlantic Ocean. However, it is slow to reproduce and there are now fewer of them due to overfishing.

The spine on the second dorsal fin is longer than the first spine.

The backbone runs all the way into the upper tail.

Slendertail lanternshark

The dark patches on the tummy of this shark contain organs, called photophores, that glow in the dark. Its lights may be for signalling to other lanternsharks.

Huge, green eyes make it possible to see in the deep, dark ocean.

» Scale

FACT FILE

» **Depth:** 200–700 m (655–2,300 ft)

» **Length:** 46 cm (18 in)

» **Fun fact:** There are more than 50 species of lanternsharks, including the smallest shark in the world.

Greenland shark

This shark lives in Arctic waters where temperatures average 2°C (36°F). It looks so dopey that it's also called a sleeper shark. A type of crustacean called a copepod often lives on the Greenland shark's eye.

This giant shark is the third biggest in the world.

» Scale

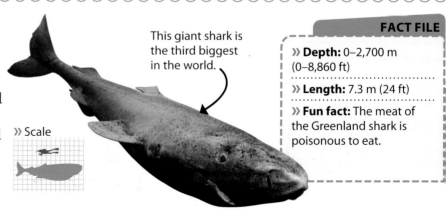

FACT FILE

» **Depth:** 0–2,700 m (0–8,860 ft)

» **Length:** 7.3 m (24 ft)

» **Fun fact:** The meat of the Greenland shark is poisonous to eat.

Each dorsal fin has a venomous spine. The spines have growth rings, like trees, and can be used to tell a dogfish's age.

Pups are born at different lengths – the **biggest mums** have the **largest babies.**

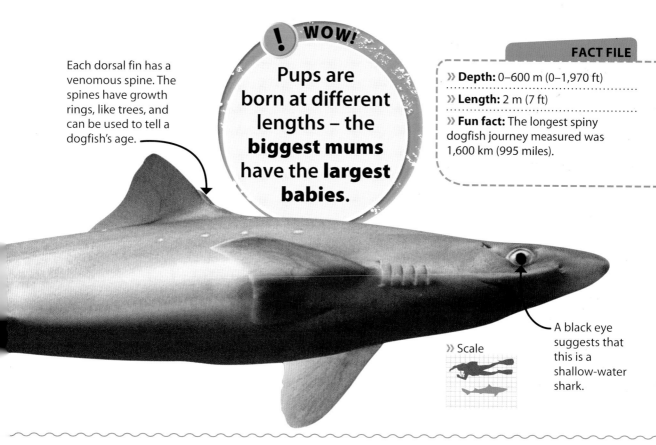

FACT FILE

» **Depth:** 0–600 m (0–1,970 ft)

» **Length:** 2 m (7 ft)

» **Fun fact:** The longest spiny dogfish journey measured was 1,600 km (995 miles).

» Scale

A black eye suggests that this is a shallow-water shark.

Prickly dogfish

This is one of five species of deepwater "rough sharks". The name refers to the large, sharpened denticles that cover their skin.

» Scale

The dorsal fins are very large and look like sails.

FACT FILE

» **Depth:** 50–1,000 m (165–3,280 ft)

» **Length:** 90 cm (35 in)

» **Fun fact:** These sharks aren't good swimmers. They rely on their oil-filled liver to help them float.

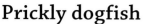

Birdbeak dogfish

The skin of this deepwater shark is armoured by large, pitchfork-shaped denticles along its sides, and it has spines on both dorsal fins. The birdbeak dogfish is a type of gulper shark.

» Scale

The very long, flat snout has lots of sense organs for finding prey in the dark.

FACT FILE

» **Depth:** 70–1,500 m (230–4,920 ft)

» **Length:** 1.1 m (4 ft)

» **Fun fact:** These sharks sometimes school in large groups, perhaps to hunt.

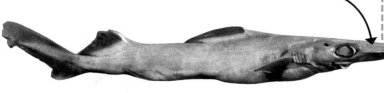

Sawsharks

These odd-looking, little sharks are unmistakeable because of their long, flat, saw-like snout. They look similar to sawfish, but the "teeth" along a sawshark's snout are thinner and sharper, and their gill slits are above their pectoral fins. There are eight types of sawshark.

Longnose sawshark

This southern Australian sawshark feeds in schools. Females give birth to litters of pups every other winter. Young sawsharks can be identified by the two or three small teeth between each large one.

» Scale

Thorny skin
The prickly shark's thin skin is protected by regularly spaced denticles. Each denticle is about 4 mm (0.2 in) across with a sharp central spine and scalloped edges.

Saw-nosed
A sawshark's snout, called a rostrum, detects vibrations and electric fields. It may be used for hunting and defence. The pair of long barbels smell and feel around for food.

Bramble sharks

There are only two species of these heavily armoured, sluggish, deepwater sharks. Their fragile skin is protected by large thorn-like scales, called denticles. When they open their huge mouth it creates a powerful suction, which pulls in unwary fish that stray too close.

Prickly shark

This shark is most common in the deep ocean, but sometimes it swims along underwater canyons into very shallow water, close to the shore. The prickly shark has been seen alone and in small groups.

» Scale

FACT FILE

» **Depth:** 4–1,100 m (13–3,610 ft)

» **Length:** 4.5 m (15 ft)

» **Fun fact:** This shark is curious when it meets divers, but it's not dangerous.

Angelsharks

These wide, flat sharks live in cold water. Angelsharks prefer habitats with sand or mud, as they like to bury themselves to hide. They lurk in ambush waiting for passing crabs and fish, and then snap them up with their huge mouth.

FACT FILE

» **Depth:** 0–130 m (0–425 ft)

» **Length:** 1.5m (5 ft)

» **Fun fact:** Angelsharks used to be called "monkfish" because, from above, they look like a hooded, robed monk.

Australian angelshark

This shark is nocturnal, which means it is active at night. During the day it lies buried in the seabed. It prefers areas near seagrass beds and rocks.

You can tell that an angelshark isn't a ray because its pectoral fins aren't attached to its head.

Bullhead sharks

There are bullhead shark fossils older than the first dinosaurs! These ancient sharks have big heads with large snouts, and crests above their eyes. Bullhead sharks live in warm water, often sleeping by day in caves or crevices and hunting shellfish at night.

The horn shark has skin that feels rough to the touch.

Bullhead sharks have two large dorsal fins with spines.

The tail has a large notch underneath it.

» Scale

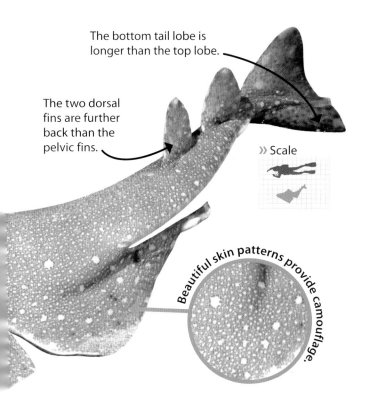

The bottom tail lobe is longer than the top lobe.

The two dorsal fins are further back than the pelvic fins.

» Scale

Beautiful skin patterns provide camouflage.

Becoming endangered

The common angelshark was once found throughout shallow seas in the northeastern Atlantic. However, so many were fished that it almost became extinct, which means there would have been none left in the world. The Canary Islands, near Morocco, are now the only place where you can still see this angelshark.

Common angelshark

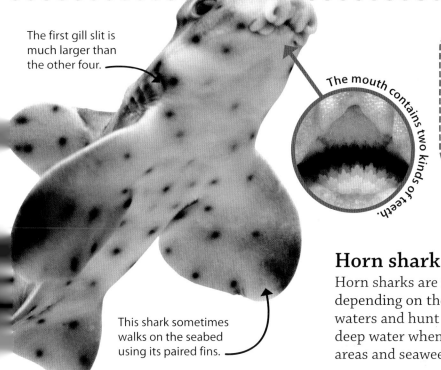

The first gill slit is much larger than the other four.

The mouth contains two kinds of teeth.

This shark sometimes walks on the seabed using its paired fins.

FACT FILE

» **Depth:** Adults 0–11 m (0–36 ft) and young 0–150 m (0–490 ft)

» **Length:** 1 m (3 ft)

» **Fun fact:** These sharks lay corkscrew-shaped eggs that they wedge into crevices in rocks to keep them safe until they hatch.

Horn shark

Horn sharks are found in different places depending on their age. Pups live in shallow waters and hunt by day, but they move to deep water when older. Adults prefer rocky areas and seaweed beds. They hunt at night.

Mackerel sharks

There are 15 species of mackerel sharks, including some of the largest, fiercest, and weirdest-looking fish in the oceans. Despite their name, these sharks don't all feed on small fish. Some slurp plankton, others hunt seals, and some scavenge on dead whales.

Long gill slits allow water to move fast over the gills underneath.

Why mackerel sharks?
Some sharks in this order like to eat small schooling fish, such as mackerel, which is how they got their name.

New teeth grow constantly to replace any gaps.

Pelagic thresher
The pelagic thresher shark lives in the open ocean. This timid shark has a small mouth to feed on small fish and sometimes squid. It is occasionally seen jumping high out of the water or, if it is really unlucky, into a boat!

» Scale

The upper part of the tail is almost as long as the body.

FACT FILE
» **Depth:** 0–550 m (0–1,800 ft)

» **Length:** 7.6 m (25 ft)

» **Fun fact:** Thresher sharks whip their tails to stun small fish to eat.

Goblin shark
This may well be the oddest shark in the world. The deepwater goblin shark's shape and colour suggest that it lives close to the seabed and swims slowly.

No other shark has a snout like this!

» Scale

FACT FILE
» **Depth:** 270–1,300 m (885–4,270 ft)

» **» Length:** 4 m (13 ft)

» **Fun fact:** The goblin shark's jaws can extend far out to grab prey.

The tall first dorsal fin can be seen when the shark swims at the surface.

» Scale

The torpedo-shaped body is very muscular.

The symmetrical tail fin indicates a very fast swimmer.

Great white shark

This predator is very smart and inquisitive. It swims constantly, migrating thousands of kilometres a year to find prey. Youngsters eat small fish, but once grown they hunt large marine mammals.

FACT FILE

» **Depth:** 0–1,300 m (0–4,270 ft)

» **Length:** 6 m (20 ft)

» **Fun fact:** This shark is warm-blooded, so its body temperature is higher than the temperature of seawater.

Basking shark

This gigantic shark filters plankton from the water to eat. It feeds at the surface in cold water, but very deeply in the warm tropics.

» Scale

Gill rakers under the gill slits sieve plankton from the water.

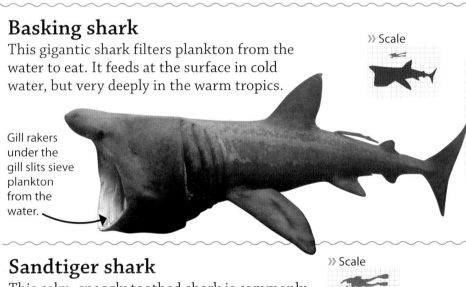

FACT FILE

» **Depth:** 0–1,200 m (0–3,940 ft)

» **Length:** 10 m (33 ft)

» **Fun fact:** This shark can filter 1.5 million litres (330,000 gallons) of water every hour.

Sandtiger shark

This calm, snaggly toothed shark is commonly displayed in aquariums. Females give birth to one large pup every one or two years.

» Scale

Sandtiger sharks gulp air to help keep themselves afloat.

FACT FILE

» **Depth:** 0–200 m (0–660 ft)

» **Length:** 3 m (10 ft)

» **Fun fact:** Sandtigers give birth to the biggest pups of any shark – they are about 1 m (3 ft) long.

Carpetsharks

There are more than 40 different types of carpetshark, including the largest fish in the world! All carpetsharks have two dorsal fins and a mouth in front of their eyes. As their name suggests, most have colourful patterns and tassel-like fringes, and many live on the seabed – just like rugs or carpets on the ocean floor.

The roughly equal top-and-bottom parts of the tail are a sign of a long-distance swimmer.

FACT FILE

» **Depth:** 0–1,000 m (0–3,280 ft)

» **Length:** 18 m (59 ft)

» **Fun fact:** These huge sharks give birth to hundreds of pups that are about 0.6 m (2 ft) long.

Blind shark

This Australian shark has tiny eyes, but it isn't actually blind. It is nocturnal, which means it feeds at night and hides in holes by day.

The small eyes close if this shark is taken out of water.

» Scale

FACT FILE

» **Depth:** 0–140 m (0–460 ft)

» **Length:** 1.2 m (4 ft)

» **Fun fact:** This hardy shark lives in surf and rock pools, and survives well in aquariums.

Nurse shark

This sociable shark sleeps in groups by day on the seabed, and hunts at night, vacuuming prey quickly into its mouth. It is often seen in aquariums.

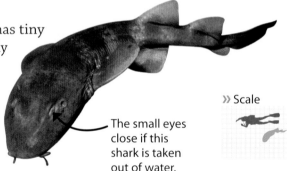

The small mouth can suck sea snails right out of their shells.

» Scale

FACT FILE

» **Depth:** 0–120 m (0–395 ft)

» **Length:** 3 m (10 ft)

» **Fun fact:** Females only give birth to pups every second year. In between, they take a rest.

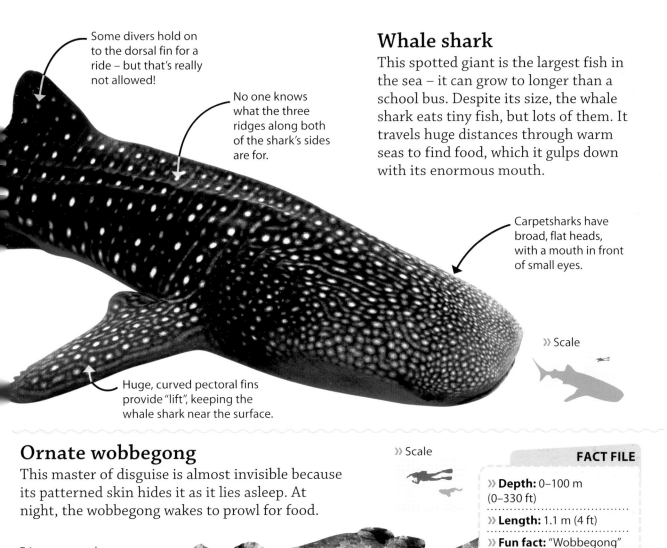

Some divers hold on to the dorsal fin for a ride – but that's really not allowed!

No one knows what the three ridges along both of the shark's sides are for.

Whale shark

This spotted giant is the largest fish in the sea – it can grow to longer than a school bus. Despite its size, the whale shark eats tiny fish, but lots of them. It travels huge distances through warm seas to find food, which it gulps down with its enormous mouth.

Carpetsharks have broad, flat heads, with a mouth in front of small eyes.

» Scale

Huge, curved pectoral fins provide "lift", keeping the whale shark near the surface.

Ornate wobbegong

This master of disguise is almost invisible because its patterned skin hides it as it lies asleep. At night, the wobbegong wakes to prowl for food.

Fringes around the mouth make it hard to see the wobbegong's outline.

» Scale

FACT FILE

» **Depth:** 0–100 m (0–330 ft)

» **Length:** 1.1 m (4 ft)

» **Fun fact:** "Wobbegong" is a native Australian word meaning "shaggy beard".

Whitespotted bamboo shark

This common tropical shark is caught for food, and often kept in aquariums. It's the only shark on this page that lays eggs instead of giving birth.

This bamboo shark has body ridges, like those on the whale shark.

» Scale

FACT FILE

» **Depth:** 0–50m (0–165 ft)

» **Length:** 1 m (3 ft)

» **Fun fact:** This bamboo shark uses its muscly pectoral fins to crawl over the seabed.

Ground sharks

Almost half of all shark species are ground sharks. Many live in deep water, but others are common in all the world's oceans. Most, such as catsharks and houndsharks, are very small, rare, and harmless. However, some are very large predators, although only a few are dangerous to people.

FACT FILE

» **Depth:** 0–80 m (0–260 ft)

» **Length:** 6 m (20 ft)

» **Fun fact:** Stingrays are the great hammerhead's favourite food, although they can defend themselves with sharp stings.

Great hammerhead

The great hammerhead is the largest of the hammerhead sharks. This species has a broad, flat head filled with sense organs for tracking down prey.

Blue shark

The world's most common oceanic shark is the blue shark. It cruises slowly along warm-water currents for thousands of kilometres, hunting for squid and small fish. Fishermen catch millions every year.

The blue shark gets its name from its blue colour.

» Scale

FACT FILE

» **Depth:** 0–350 m (0–1,150 ft)

» **Length:** 3.8 m (13 ft)

» **Fun fact:** Divers use bait to attract blue sharks for cage diving.

Blacktip reef shark

This strong swimmer always hangs out on Indo-Pacific reefs, where it is popular with divers. It is sometimes also kept in aquariums.

» Scale

The black fin tip has a white base.

FACT FILE

» **Depth:** 0–20 m (0–65 ft)

» **Length:** 2 m (7 ft)

» **Fun fact:** Some of these sharks have swum all the way through the Suez Canal, from the Red Sea to the Mediterranean.

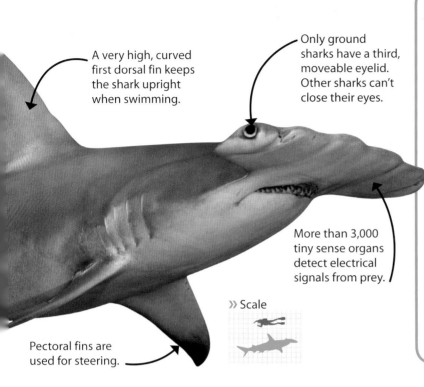

A very high, curved first dorsal fin keeps the shark upright when swimming.

Only ground sharks have a third, moveable eyelid. Other sharks can't close their eyes.

More than 3,000 tiny sense organs detect electrical signals from prey.

Pectoral fins are used for steering.

» Scale

Huge hammer

The broad, flattened head of a hammerhead improves swimming control and "lift", which pushes the shark up in the water. Widely separated nostrils help the shark to pinpoint the source of food smells. The winghead shark has a head width almost half the length of its whole body!

X-ray of a winghead shark

Pyjama shark

The pyjama shark is a sort of "catshark". Named for their stripes, these sharks are only found in the waters around the tip of South Africa, where they live in surf, caves, and other rocky areas.

The pyjama shark's dorsal fins are both close to its tail.

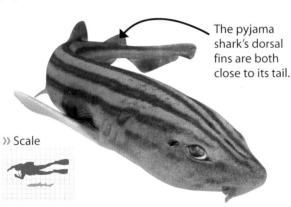

» Scale

FACT FILE

» **Depth:** 0–100 m (0–330 ft)

» **Length:** 1 m (3 ft)

» **Fun fact:** These sharks lay pairs of eggs, which hatch on the seabed.

Leopard shark

Despite its name, this shark is from the "houndshark" family. It lives in large schools, in shallow water on the Pacific coast of the USA and Mexico.

The lower tail lobe is much smaller than the upper one.

» Scale

FACT FILE

» **Depth:** 0–20 m (0–65 ft)

» **Length:** 2 m (7 ft)

» **Fun fact:** Females give birth to their pups in water only 1 m (3 ft) deep.

Skeleton

A shark's skeleton is not made of bone. Instead it is made of light, flexible cartilage. This is the same material that your ears and nose are made of, but stronger. There aren't many parts to a shark's skeleton, just a skull, jaws, spine, gill arches, and supports underneath the fins.

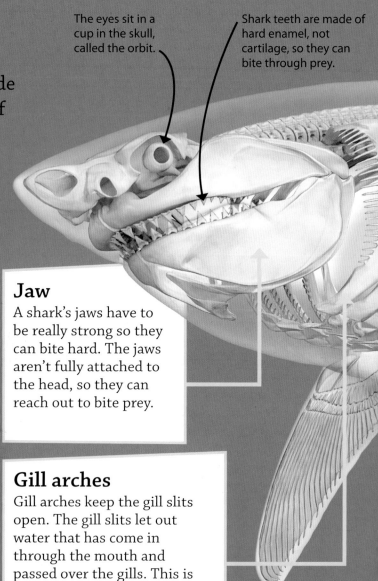

The eyes sit in a cup in the skull, called the orbit.

Shark teeth are made of hard enamel, not cartilage, so they can bite through prey.

Great white shark skeleton

A shark's body is supported by the water around it, so its skeleton can be bendier than a human's. However, in very old, large sharks, the cartilage becomes much harder and more similar to bone.

Jaw

A shark's jaws have to be really strong so they can bite hard. The jaws aren't fully attached to the head, so they can reach out to bite prey.

Gill arches

Gill arches keep the gill slits open. The gill slits let out water that has come in through the mouth and passed over the gills. This is how a shark breathes.

Movement

The great white shark swims fast by beating just the end of its tail. Long, thin sharks such as this dogfish swim slowly, like an eel, using most of their body length.

Stiff fins push against the water, helping the shark swim.

The tail, which contains zig-zag bands of muscle, is more than half the length of this shark.

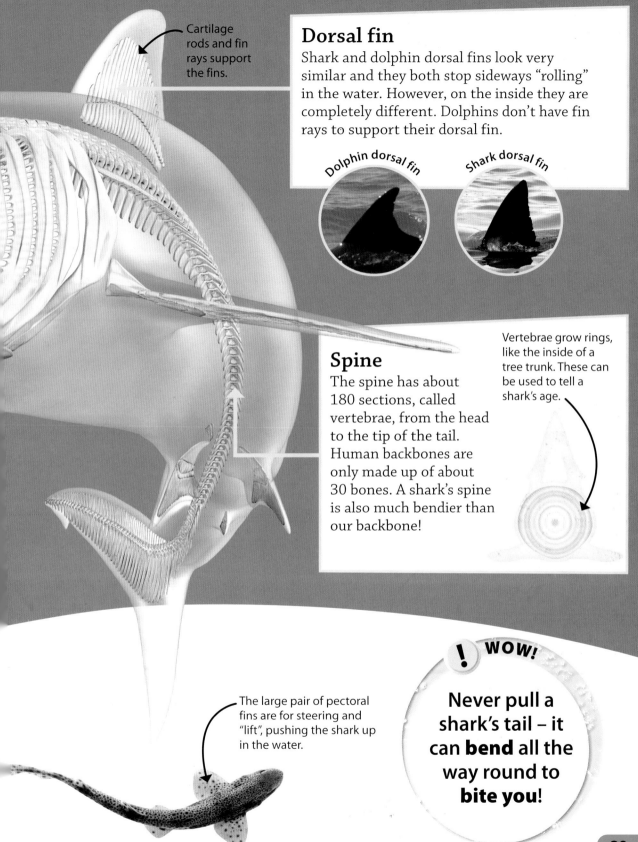

Cartilage rods and fin rays support the fins.

Dorsal fin

Shark and dolphin dorsal fins look very similar and they both stop sideways "rolling" in the water. However, on the inside they are completely different. Dolphins don't have fin rays to support their dorsal fin.

Dolphin dorsal fin

Shark dorsal fin

Spine

The spine has about 180 sections, called vertebrae, from the head to the tip of the tail. Human backbones are only made up of about 30 bones. A shark's spine is also much bendier than our backbone!

Vertebrae grow rings, like the inside of a tree trunk. These can be used to tell a shark's age.

The large pair of pectoral fins are for steering and "lift", pushing the shark up in the water.

! WOW!

Never pull a shark's tail – it can **bend** all the way round to **bite you!**

Inside a shark

Beneath a shark's skin are hidden all the important parts it needs to survive. Its muscles are attached to the inside of the thick skin itself, not to the skeleton, like ours are. Underneath the muscles, the organs all play a vital role in keeping the shark swimming.

Stomach

The J-shaped stomach mainly stores food. The shark can turn this inside out, through its mouth, to spit out inedible stuff that was eaten by mistake!

Dorsal fin

Brain

Shark brains come in many different shapes and sizes, depending upon the senses the type of shark uses most. Nerves run from the brain to all parts of the body.

Liver

A shark's liver is enormous, about 25–30 per cent of its body weight! It is full of oil, which is very light – lighter than water. This helps the shark to stay afloat.

Pectoral fin
(one of two)

Gills

Water comes in through the mouth and goes out over the gills, which collect oxygen for the shark to breathe. Some sharks can't breathe if they stop swimming. Others can pump water over their gills as they lie on the seabed.

Heart

There are two main chambers in a shark's heart. One chamber has thick, strong walls, to pump blood through the gills and all around the body. The other one collects returning blood.

Kidneys

Sharks aren't waterproof! Water seeps in through their gills and skin. The kidneys collect and get rid of unwanted water.

Denticles on the skin

Skin

Shark skin is really thick. It is also covered in hard scales called denticles. These tiny interlocking teeth protect the skin and also streamline it, helping the shark to swim faster.

Second dorsal fin

Tail fin

Anal fin

Pelvic fin (one of two)

Warm-blooded

Muscles get hot when they work hard, but this heat is quickly lost through the gills and skin. Most sharks are cold-blooded, but some sharks have a system that lets their warm blood heat any cool blood returning from the gills and skin, to keep themselves warm inside. This makes them faster-growing and more efficient hunters.

Intestine

This is where food is digested. A shark's intestine is curled into a very tight spiral, making it look much shorter and fatter than a mammal's long intestines.

Salmon sharks live in the North Pacific Ocean.

Shark eggs

Many sharks lay leathery eggs in nursery grounds – safe places where shark mothers can anchor their eggs to the seabed. The pups inside live off a yolk sac while they grow into miniature copies of their parents – it may take up to a year before they are ready to hatch. Many rays and all chimaeras are also egg-layers.

Types of eggs

Sharks and their relatives lay eggs in pairs, but each species has different-shaped eggs. An empty, washed-up egg case is called a "mermaid's purse". It has an opening where the pup wriggled out.

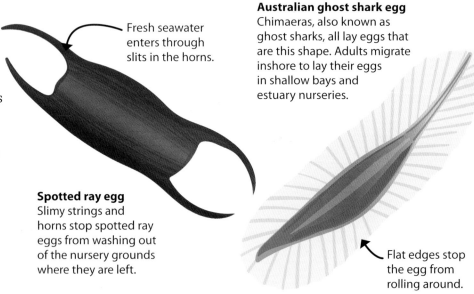

Fresh seawater enters through slits in the horns.

Australian ghost shark egg
Chimaeras, also known as ghost sharks, all lay eggs that are this shape. Adults migrate inshore to lay their eggs in shallow bays and estuary nurseries.

Spotted ray egg
Slimy strings and horns stop spotted ray eggs from washing out of the nursery grounds where they are left.

Flat edges stop the egg from rolling around.

Hatching

The embryo of a growing shark, ray, or chimaera curls up to fit inside its egg case. Its tail pumps in fresh seawater so it can breathe, but it stops if it senses danger. When its yolk is finished, the baby wriggles out.

An undulate ray hatches from its egg case.

The pup uncurls its fins as it escapes.

Live birth

About 60 per cent of sharks give birth to pups, rather than laying eggs. Some pups are born soon after hatching from eggs inside their mother. Others hatch earlier, and feed on spare eggs before birth. A few sharks have placentas, like mammals, which connect the mother to the pup and provide them with food.

A lemon shark pup being born

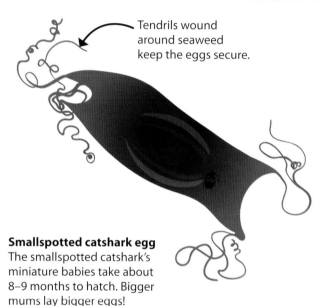

Tendrils wound around seaweed keep the eggs secure.

Smallspotted catshark egg
The smallspotted catshark's miniature babies take about 8–9 months to hatch. Bigger mums lay bigger eggs!

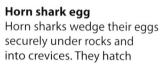

Horn shark egg
Horn sharks wedge their eggs securely under rocks and into crevices. They hatch 7–9 months later.

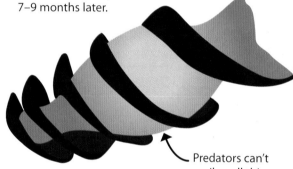

Predators can't easily pull this screw-shaped egg out of its crevice.

Free at last! The empty egg case may wash up on a beach nearby.

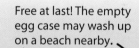

! WOW!

Shark **egg cases** are made from the same material, called keratin, as your **hair and fingernails!**

33

Baby sharks

Mother sharks never look after their young, and growing up is a dangerous time. Big sharks often like eating little ones! Many pups spend a few years hiding in places that big sharks can't reach. Others use a disguise to avoid being spotted by hungry predators.

Lemon shark nursery
A mother lemon shark gives birth in the place where she grew up safely. This warm lagoon in the Bahamas provides shelter and food for lots of pups. They will spend four years living here with many brothers, sisters, and cousins.

WOW!

Baby sharks are born with **teeth**, ready to **hunt**.

Stay away

Shark pups sometimes look very different from their parents, not just in size but also in shape and colour. Pups are often camouflaged, which means their appearance makes them hard to spot. A few pups disguise themselves as completely different animals.

Adult zebra shark
Adult zebra sharks have spots – they don't look like a zebra at all! Only youngsters have stripes, as well as long, thin bodies.

Zebra shark pup
These pups have black and white stripes, but these aren't to help them hide. They make the pups look like dangerous sea snakes.

Sea snake
The stripes on this sea snake warn that it's venomous. Baby zebra sharks even swim like sea snakes so that predators stay clear!

Nursery features

Safety
This nursery ground is a warm lagoon. Pups swim far into it, where it's much too shallow for adult sharks or big fish to hunt. The roots of mangrove trees provide safe hiding places for baby sharks.

Food
The lagoon and mangroves are full of little fish for the pups to eat. As they grow older, they start hunting bigger fish in slightly deeper water.

Friends
Scientists studying baby lemon sharks in their nurseries have discovered that pups are often found with the same companions. They even have individual personalities – some are timid, but others are much braver.

Social sharks

Many sharks live in groups, called schools. Schools usually contain sharks of the same species and size, but not always. When living side by side, these sharks need to be able to communicate with each other about food and mates.

Types of behaviour

Sharks need to cooperate when they are hunting together, looking for a mate, or to avoid fights. They use different signals to let each other know what they mean.

Schooling

Sharks may swim together all the time, or only at particular times during the day or year. Head-flicking and swimming in spirals in these groups may let other sharks know to keep out of the way. These behaviours may also be done to impress a mate.

Scalloped hammerhead sharks schooling

Getting along

When different shark species school together, they must be able to understand each other's signals.

A great hammerhead and a nurse shark swim together

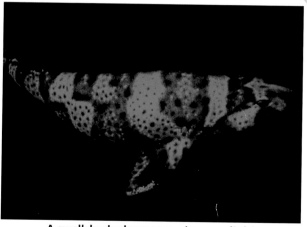

A swellshark glows green in moonlight

Glow-in-the-dark shark

This swellshark absorbs moonlight to make its skin glow. Humans can't see this light without special cameras, but other swellsharks can. Scientists haven't yet decoded this secret signal.

Body language

Sharks can't talk, but they can use their body position to communicate with each other. Many shark behaviours are used to decide who is bigger and stronger. This can prevent fights, as smaller sharks will avoid larger sharks, or show who would make the best mate.

Size display
A size display shows which out of two sharks is larger – bigger sharks are in charge. The biggest sharks get to swim in the middle of a school, while smaller ones have to hang out at the edges.

Splashing
Tail slaps are common when several great white sharks are feeding together. The sharks may be trying to scare each other away from their food.

Swim-by
A slow swim-by is a good way to check out another shark. This gives sharks a chance to see if they know one another.

Circling
Sometimes sharks circle each other before feeding in a group. They might be deciding who gets to start first.

WARNING!

Hunching
A hunched back, with the head up, and fins pointed down means "Stay away from me! I'll bite if you come closer!".

1

Squid

2

Crab

3 Tuna

Port Jackson shark teeth

Basking shark mouth

Shortfin mako shark teeth

A **Port Jackson shark**
Sharp teeth at the front grab prey, while rounded pads at the back grind up tough food.

B **Basking shark**
Filter feeders use gill rakers to sieve out their tiny food from seawater.

C **Shortfin mako shark**
Needle-like teeth pointing backwards mean slippery prey can't escape this shark.

Dinnertime

It is possible to guess what sharks prefer to eat from the shape of their teeth – particularly if they are choosy. Some sharks catch and swallow their dinner whole. Others have jagged teeth like knives that cut up larger prey. A few have grinding teeth for smashing up tough shells.

Conveyor-belt teeth

Sharks lose all their teeth every month or two, but a replacement set moves forwards right away.

Sandtiger sharks replace one tooth every two days – that's more than 10,000 in a lifetime!

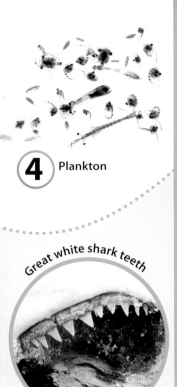

4 Plankton

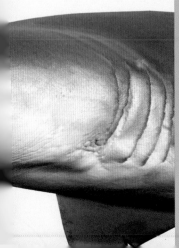

Great white shark teeth

D Great white shark

Jagged, pointed teeth bite out chunks of large prey for this shark to swallow.

Big teeth

Big teeth are used to bite chunks out of animals that are too large to be swallowed whole. The biggest-ever shark teeth are from the prehistoric shark Megalodon. These teeth are 18 cm (7 in) long.

Megalodon tooth
This tooth is between 2 and 16 million years old. It is a fossil from a huge Megalodon. This shark probably ate whales.

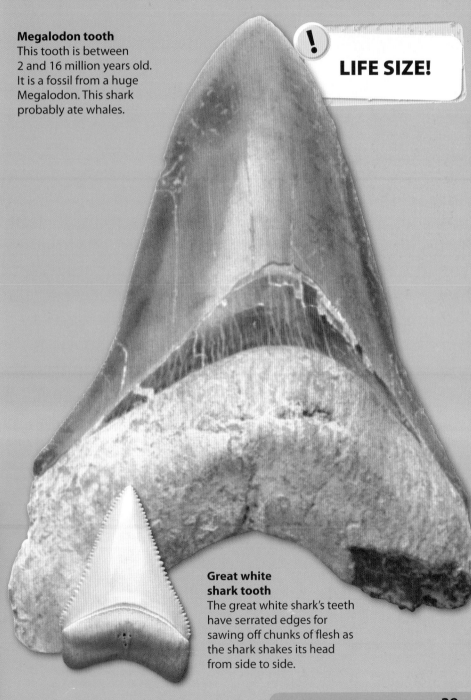

! **LIFE SIZE!**

Great white shark tooth
The great white shark's teeth have serrated edges for sawing off chunks of flesh as the shark shakes its head from side to side.

Surprise attack

Great white sharks suprise prey by attacking from below. Tourist boats in South Africa tow model seals to encourage the sharks to breach out of the sea – don't try this yourself!

The eye is rolled back to avoid being damaged by prey during an attack.

Hunting

There are no vegetarian sharks! All of them are hunters, but they catch their dinner in different ways. Some sharks dig for shellfish in the sandy seabed, while others hide and ambush passing prey. The fastest swimmers chase down squid and fish, grabbing them with razor-sharp teeth.

! WOW!

Many sharks **change** tooth shape and their favourite food as they grow.

Test bite
This shark is "mouthing" a boat's engine to decide whether it's good enough to eat. Sharks often give objects a test bite to find out whether they are edible.

Galapagos shark

Blacktip reef sharks

Cooperative
Some sharks hunt in packs, working together to herd, confuse, and capture shoaling prey that would escape a lone hunter.

Cookiecutter shark

Quick bite
Light given out by these tiny sharks may attract larger predators. If the predators get too close they can end up losing a cookie-shaped mouthful of flesh to these little monsters.

Australian angelshark

Ambush
Flat sharks use their patterned skin and a light covering of sand for camouflage. They hide and wait for unwary prey to swim too close, then jump out at them.

Filter feeders

The world's biggest sharks feed on the smallest animals – plankton. Because plankton are tiny, they have to be filtered out of seawater – teeth are useless! Filter feeders use their gills to trap plankton, as well as for breathing.

Whale shark
This shark stops swimming to take huge gulps of water. It closes its mouth to push the water over its gills, straining out the plankton and squeezing the excess water out of its gill slits, before swallowing its catch.

Plankton

Plankton includes all sorts of tiny swimming and floating animals, including crabs and other shellfish, miniature eggs, and baby fish.

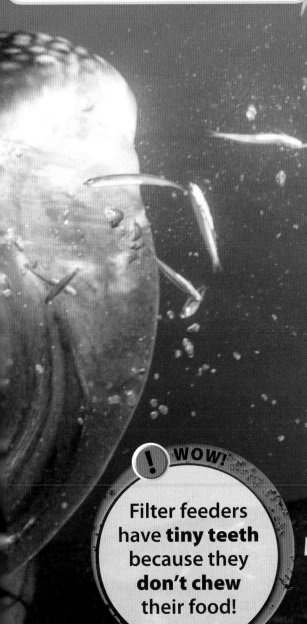

Gentle giants

Divers love swimming with these huge sharks because they don't have big teeth or bite, and aren't dangerous.

Basking shark with mouth open, showing open gill slits

Basking shark

The basking shark is a "ram feeder" – it never stops swimming and lets water pass over its gills continuously. It collects minute plankton at the surface and in deep water.

Photographs of megamouth sharks are rare because they live in very deep water.

Megamouth shark

This deepwater plankton eater has never been seen feeding, but probably gulps mouthfuls of water, like the whale shark.

! WOW!

Filter feeders have **tiny teeth** because they **don't chew** their food!

Human senses

A human's five senses are sight, hearing, smell, taste, and touch. Our sense organs detect signals such as light, noise, and pressure, and then send messages to the brain, which tells the body how to react.

Hearing
Our ears collect sound, which travels to internal sense organs that detect vibrations – and gravity.

Sight
A lens inside our eyes focuses light onto special cells that detect light and colour.

Smell
The inside of the nose is full of tiny cells that can detect thousands of different smells!

Senses

Animals need senses to find out about the world. They are essential for locating food and avoiding danger. Signals are detected by sense organs. Most sense organs are on the head, but one covers the whole body – it's the skin! Sharks have the same five main senses as us, but some are higher-powered than ours. They also have an amazing sixth sense – they can detect electricity.

Taste
Taste buds on top of our tongues detect salty, sweet, bitter, sour, and savoury tastes.

Touch
The skin is our biggest sense organ. It detects pressure, or touch, and temperature.

Taste
Sharks have taste cells inside their mouths and on their barbels – if they have them.

Electroreception
This extra sense detects tiny electric fields from living animals and the Earth's magnetic field. It helps sharks to find food and navigate through huge oceans.

Smell
Sharks have a fantastic sense of smell. They don't use their nostrils for anything else!

Sight
The eyes of sharks living in shallow, clear water are very like ours. Deepwater sharks need huge eyes to capture the tiniest glimmer of light.

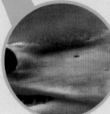

Hearing
It's almost impossible to see the tiny openings leading to a shark's ears. On the inside, they are very like ours.

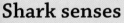

Shark senses

Five of a shark's senses are like ours, but they have a special sixth sense called electroreception. Sharks can also sense touch without being in contact with an object, using special receptors down the side of their body.

Lateral line
The lateral line can be found running along the sides of sharks and other fish. Tiny organs inside it detect pressure changes in the water – a remote sense of touch. This helps them find moving prey.

Sensing electricity

Sharks have an amazing super-sense, called electroreception. They use special cells, known as ampullae, scattered under their head and around their mouth to detect electricity. All animals produce tiny amounts of electricity, and electroreception can pick this up. Electroreception is also useful to help a shark find its way on long journeys, as it can identify the direction of the Earth's magnetic field.

Hunting rays

Sharks use their eyes, nose and electric sense organs to find prey. Scent is a long-distance clue and sight is useful closer up, but electroreception is important when prey is only centimetres away – even when it's hidden from view.

! WOW!

Deepwater sharks **chew** underwater **phone cables** because the wires produce **electric fields**!

Torpedo ray

Torpedo rays generate electricity in special cells. They store it in "battery" organs and then release it as electric shocks to stun prey or for defence. A common torpedo ray can produce 200 volts. Ancient Greek doctors used electric rays to shock patients for pain relief, but don't try this at home!

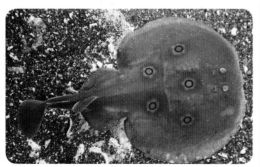

Common torpedo ray

Electric field

All animals' muscles produce tiny pulses of electricity that form electric fields. Electricity travels well through salty water, so sharks can pick it up to find hidden fish.

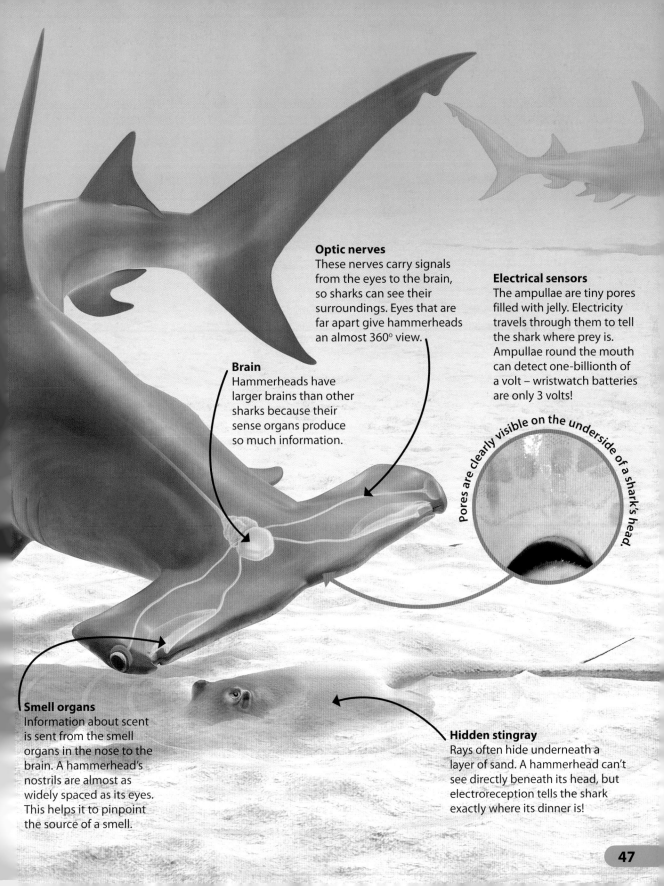

Optic nerves
These nerves carry signals from the eyes to the brain, so sharks can see their surroundings. Eyes that are far apart give hammerheads an almost 360° view.

Brain
Hammerheads have larger brains than other sharks because their sense organs produce so much information.

Electrical sensors
The ampullae are tiny pores filled with jelly. Electricity travels through them to tell the shark where prey is. Ampullae round the mouth can detect one-billionth of a volt – wristwatch batteries are only 3 volts!

Pores are clearly visible on the underside of a shark's head.

Smell organs
Information about scent is sent from the smell organs in the nose to the brain. A hammerhead's nostrils are almost as widely spaced as its eyes. This helps it to pinpoint the source of a smell.

Hidden stingray
Rays often hide underneath a layer of sand. A hammerhead can't see directly beneath its head, but electroreception tells the shark exactly where its dinner is!

Where do sharks live?

Sharks live almost everywhere under water. They are found in the open ocean, shallow and deep seas, and even some rivers. However, most kinds of shark choose to live in one particular part of the ocean. You may even need to watch out on land – the epaulette shark can sometimes be found walking on the shoreline!

The walking shark

The epaulette shark of New Guinea and Australia is able to survive out of water for short periods of time. It scuttles between rock pools on its muscular fins. However, the shore can be dangerous and it has two large eyespots near its pectoral fins to scare predators away.

Epaulette shark

Freshwater

It is rare for sharks to live in freshwater. The only ones that do live in warm, tropical rivers. A few species can adjust to changing salt levels, and travel back and forth between freshwater and the sea.

Coast

Many small, harmless sharks spend their entire lives in the shallow water near the shore. Some may live unseen just a few metres away from holidaymakers.

Coral reef

Coral reefs provide habitats filled with food in otherwise empty tropical seas. Sharks use the reefs as homes, or may visit occasionally to hunt for food.

Open ocean

Oceans are home to long-distance travellers. Some sharks commute daily from the surface to a depth of 500 m (1,640 ft) and travel thousands of kilometres a year.

Seafloor

The sharks that live in this rich feeding ground don't need to travel far to eat. The seafloor is home to many types of shark that never move far away from the sandy bottom.

Deep sea

Very little light reaches this cold, barren habitat. It is home to sharks that can glow in the dark, and others with huge, green eyes that can see the slightest glimmer of light.

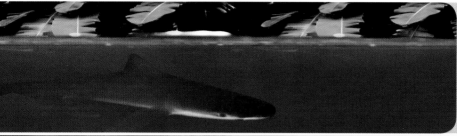

Bull shark
Young bull sharks are most likely to be found in rivers. They may use them as freshwater nurseries. Adults sometimes bite unwary river swimmers.

Nursehound
This spotty shark winds its eggs onto seaweed in very shallow water. It may even be found by people paddling at low tide!

Whitetip reef shark
These stout sharks often sleep by day, but gather in packs to hunt at night. They search out dozing fish that are hidden in the coral.

Oceanic whitetip shark
This large, inquisitive animal never stops swimming. Once a very common oceanic shark, it's now under threat from fishing.

Australian angelshark
Angelsharks can hide perfectly on the sandy bottom of the seafloor. This means they can stay still, waiting for prey to come to them.

Bigeye houndshark
These little sharks live in the very deep waters of the Red Sea and Indian Ocean. They need huge eyes to catch small fish and squid in the dark.

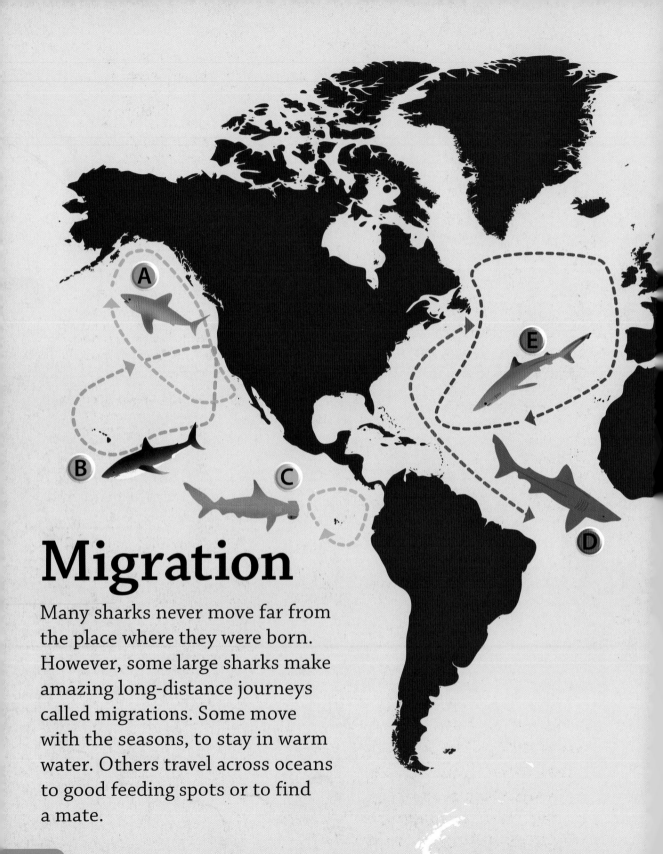

Migration

Many sharks never move far from the place where they were born. However, some large sharks make amazing long-distance journeys called migrations. Some move with the seasons, to stay in warm water. Others travel across oceans to good feeding spots or to find a mate.

MIGRATION ROUTES

A **Salmon sharks** These warm-blooded sharks prefer cold water. They swim between the coasts of California and Alaska, USA, and out to the middle of the North Pacific Ocean.

B **Great white sharks** Great white sharks spend the summer in California, USA, then swim 4,000 km (2,490 miles) to Hawaii for the winter, then go back again.

C **Scalloped hammerheads** Hammerheads may use their electric sense to follow underwater magnetic highways between the islands of Malpelo, Cocos, and the Galapagos.

D **Basking sharks** These sharks don't like warm water. They feed on the surface in the North Atlantic, but dive very deep to cross the equator.

E **Blue sharks** Blue sharks use an ocean current, called the North Atlantic Drift, to help them swim clockwise around the Atlantic Ocean.

F **Whale sharks** It may take two or three years for a whale shark to travel around an ocean, visiting feeding grounds along the way.

G **Shortfin makos** A shortfin mako named Carol swam from New Zealand to Fiji and back, and then out to Tonga, all in one year!

REALLY?

Great white sharks meet in an empty patch of ocean near Hawaii called the **"white shark café"**, probably to find a mate!

Interview with...

We put some questions to Rob Allen, a shark conservationist, photographer, and adventurer. He travels the world diving with sharks and working to help protect them from the threat of extinction.

Q: We know it is something to do with sharks, but what do you actually do?

A: I lead scuba-diving expeditions to remote parts of the world to dive with and photograph sharks.

Q: What made you decide to become a photographer and conservationist?

A: I have always loved photography and the sea – photographing sharks was a natural way to combine these. I have been a shark conservationist for about 20 years, since learning how dangerously close to extinction most shark species are. Back then, most people didn't care about saving sharks, but the tide is turning now, with many people far more interested in conservation.

Q: Is your job dangerous?

A: Sharks are wild animals, and so you have to be very careful around some of the larger ones. However, if you take the right precautions and have someone watching your back (they do like to creep up on you) then it is safe. I have done over 600 shark dives and never felt threatened – not by the sharks at least; as there are some pretty aggressive fish, too.

Q: What sort of equipment do you use?

A: I have a Canon 5D Digital SLR camera that is put in a solid metal case so I can take it underwater. Two big strobe lights, which produce a quick flash, help to light up the water when it's dark. I use wide angle lenses, which means I have to get very close to the sharks.

Q: What are the best and worst parts of your job?

A: Every shark encounter is fantastic and it's a real privilege to be with them in their environment. Unfortunately, the sea and weather can't be controlled and I have spent many hours on boats in storms – luckily I don't get seasick.

Great hammerhead shark

Great white shark

Rob scuba-diving with a great hammerhead shark

Q: What is the most exciting thing you have ever photographed?

A: I love the annual Sardine Run off the coast of South Africa, where millions of fish are herded into large bait balls by dolphins. All the marine predators are attracted, including sharks, whales, sea lions, and gannets, which plunge in to feast. Being close to all that energy and action is incredibly exciting.

Q: What are the biggest problems facing sharks and what can you do to help them?

A: Many types of shark are close to extinction. As the top predators in the ocean, they are essential for a healthy ecosystem, as they keep fish populations in balance. You can help by understanding the conservation issues and educating others. Also avoid buying shark products like teeth necklaces.

Q: Do you have a favourite type of shark?

A: That's a difficult question. Blue sharks are the prettiest sharks, bull sharks have the most attitude, and great whites are magnificent and make you feel totally insignificant, but my favourites are tiger sharks as they have so much character.

Tiger shark

Sharks in danger

Scientists estimate that about one quarter of all shark species are in danger. Millions of sharks are killed each year. The biggest sharks and those that live in shallow coastal water are at greatest risk. If sharks are overfished or lose their habitats they could face extinction. Many conservationists, however, work to protect sharks and try to stop their numbers from dropping too far.

Trophy hunting

Many anglers like to catch sharks, but most put them back in the sea alive. Trophy hunters kill big sharks for their jaws and teeth, or to weigh, measure, and photograph them during fishing competitions.

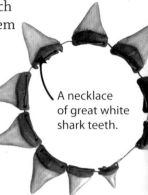

A necklace of great white shark teeth.

PRODUCTS

Many sharks have meat that can be eaten, and their fins are used in soup. Sometimes when a shark's fins are removed the rest of it is thrown away. People also use sharks' thick skin for leather, oil from their livers for make-up, and cartilage in pills.

Shark fin soup is sometimes eaten at banquets in East Asia.

OVERFISHING

This is the greatest threat to sharks. Some are hunted for food and others for parts to make products, such as oil. Sharks are caught with a hook and line or with nets. They can also be killed accidentally by fishermen trying to catch other fish.

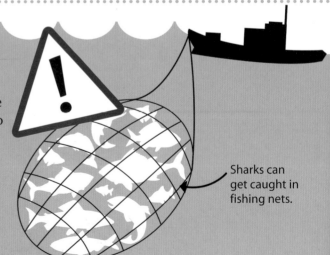

Sharks can get caught in fishing nets.

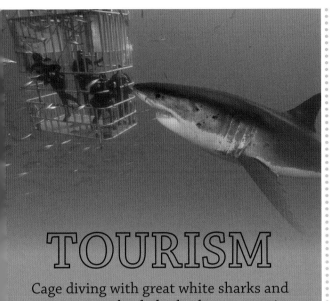

TOURISM

Cage diving with great white sharks and swimming with whale sharks are amazing experiences. They also bring lots of people and money to coastal areas. However, they should be organised carefully so that sharks aren't disturbed or harmed.

Conservation

Many people support shark conservation. Some join organisations for saving marine wildlife, while scientists carry out research to learn about the lives of sharks and how to help them. Managers of fisheries try to make sure catches are sustainable, which limits the number of sharks caught.

Electronic tags track sharks so scientists can learn more about them.

Habitat loss

Some sharks only live in shallow coastal areas, or have nursery grounds there. Unfortunately many people live right next door. Coastal habitats are often used for housing, ports, and industrial development. Sharks have nowhere else to go!

This mangrove forest, a lemon shark nursery, is having a hotel built on it.

POLLUTION

Marine litter can entangle and harm wildlife. Sometimes it's eaten by sharks and other sea animals. Invisible pollution, such as chemical waste, is also dangerous. Sharks can live for a long time and can build up enough toxic chemicals to make them bad for us to eat.

Shark facts and figures

Sharks are a fascinating group of fish. Here are some weird and wonderful facts you might not know about them!

Tiger sharks have been found to eat **cans, shoes, and even licence plates from cars!**

The whale shark has

OPEN WIDE!

Sharks let fish called remoras clean parasites from their skin, even inside their mouths, without eating them!

SHY SHARK

When threatened, the shy shark curls into a protective ring.

99 days

A great white shark called Nicole travelled 11,100 km (6,900 miles) from Australia to South Africa in 99 days.

100 million

sharks are killed by people a year.

GALEOPHOBIA

is the fear of sharks.

Baby sandtiger sharks have been known to eat each other while still inside their mother!

the **thickest** skin of any animal.

Bull sharks are one of the most **dangerous** species of shark, along with **great white sharks** and **tiger sharks**.

500

m (1,640 ft) is how far male great white sharks swim down and up to impress females.

400

Greenland sharks can live as long as 400 years.

1976

The megamouth shark wasn't discovered until 1976.

Top sharks

You've read this far, so you already know that sharks are amazing animals! Here are a few more facts that you can use to astonish your friends. Find out which shark is the fastest, which can jump the highest, and which lives the deepest.

Highest leaper

Sharks jump to show how strong they are, or, when they are swimming too fast to stop! A jump can also knock off a parasite, such as a blood-sucking copepod (a type of crustacean) or a fisherman's hook.

6 m (20 ft)

Shortfin mako
This shark has to swim very fast to jump that high!

3 m (10 ft)

Thresher shark
A thresher shark may jump several times in a row. Even their long tail clears the water.

2.5 m (8 ft)

Great white shark
Great white sharks breach when charging from deep water to hit prey swimming on the surface.

32 kph (20 mph)

Blue shark
The blue shark usually glides slowly around oceans, but it can sprint much faster.

Fastest swimmer

A shark must be very fast to eat fast food (meaning speedy fish, not burgers). Otherwise they need to be very good at sneaking up on their dinner, ambushing it.

56 kph (35 mph)

Shortfin mako shark
The shortfin mako is the world's fastest shark. It can catch fast prey such as tuna.

40 kph (25 mph)

Great white shark
This shark reaches its top speed when chasing prey. It often surprises its dinner from below.

Deepest living

The sharks here have been fished up from very deep water. Other types of shark might live or dive even deeper – but no one has yet caught them doing it.

Cookiecutter shark
In third place is the cookiecutter shark. This tiny predator sneaks up on prey in the dark. It has the biggest teeth for its size of any shark.

3,500 m (11,480 ft)

Portuguese dogfish
Runner-up is the Portuguese dogfish. It bites chunks out of its prey like the cookiecutter does.

3,675 m (12,060 ft)

Great lanternshark
The deep-diving champion is the great lanternshark. This shark shines its light in the dark depths.

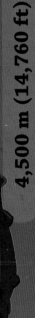

4,500 m (14,760 ft)

Glossary

Here are the meanings of some words that are useful for you to know when learning about sharks.

adaptation Way in which an animal becomes better suited to its habitat

ampullae Special jelly-filled pores that detect electricity

anal fin Single fin underneath a shark's body, near the tail

ancestor Animal to which a more recent animal is related

armour Naturally hard body covering that provides protection for an animal

barbels Feelers near a shark's nostrils, or on the rostrum of a sawshark

breach When an animal makes a complete, or almost complete, leap out of the water and splashes back

camouflage Colours or patterns on an animal's skin that help it merge with the environment

carnivore Animal that eats only meat

cartilage A tough but flexible material that makes up the skeletons of sharks and their relatives

chimaera Unusual type of fish related to sharks. Also called ghost sharks and ratfish

cold-blooded Animal with a body temperature that goes up and down to match the surrounding air or water temperature

conservation Trying to stop an animal or plant from becoming extinct

courtship Special types of animal behaviour that are used to attract a mate

denticle Small, tooth-like scale found on the skin of sharks and rays

dorsal fin Fin on the back of a shark. There may be one or two, with or without a spine in front of it

ecosystem A living community of plants and animals found together, and their environment

egg case Tough, outer capsule that protects a developing shark, ray, or chimaera

elasmobranchs Sharks, rays, guitarfish, and sawfish

electroreception Sharks' ability to sense electricity

environment Surroundings in which an animal lives

estuary End of a river where freshwater meets the sea

extinction When all of a particular animal species dies out and there are none left in the world

A great white shark breaching

filter feeding When small animals in water are sieved out with gill rakers and eaten

Leopard shark snout

gill rakers Small, hard projections on a shark's gills that filter small food items from the water

gills Organs that allow fish to breath underwater

gill slits Openings that allow the water that comes in through a shark's mouth to pass out over the gills

habitat Natural home environment of an animal

lagoon Area of shallow water partly or completely enclosed by a barrier of land

mangrove Tree that grows in shallow sea water

marine Describes animals that live in the sea, their habitat, and environment

migration Regular movement of animals, often to feed or breed

nocturnal Animals that are awake at night, when they hunt or feed

nursery ground Area, often in a shallow sheltered place, where newborn sharks live

parasite Animal that lives on or inside another animal and feeds off it

pectoral fins First pair of large fins underneath a shark. In skates and rays they are joined to the head to form wings

pelvic fins Second pair of fins underneath a shark, before the tail

poison Harmful substance released by an animal that may be deadly if touched or eaten

polar Areas near the North and South poles

predator Animal that hunts other living animals for food

prey Animal that is hunted for food

pup Newborn or newly hatched young of a shark or ray

reproduce To have young. Sharks and rays may lay eggs or give birth to live young

rostrum Long part of a shark's snout. It is flattened and edged with teeth in sawsharks and sawfish

snout Part of the head in front of an animal's eyes and mouth

species Specific types of animal with shared features that can mate and produce young together

temperate Area or climate with mild temperatures

tropical Area or climate with hot temperatures

venom Harmful substance that may be deadly if injected into the skin by a sting

warm-blooded Animal that keeps a constant body temperature

Index

Acknowledgments

The publisher would like to thank the following people for their assistance in the preparation of this book: Ann Cannings, Abi Wright, Surya Deogun, Suzena Sengupta, Garima Sharma, and Nand Kishor Acharya for design assistance, Arran Lewis for CGI artwork, Polly Goodman for proofreading, and Helen Peters for compiling the index. The publisher would also like to thank Gill Pitts and Jolyon Goddard for editorial assistance and Rob Allen for the "Interview with…" interview.

The publisher would like to thank the following for their kind permission to reproduce their photographs:

(Key: a-above; b-below/bottom; c-centre; f-far; l-left; r-right; t-top)

1 Alamy Stock Photo: Brandon Cole Marine Photography. 2 Getty Images: Wayne Lynch / All Canada Photos. 3 Alamy Stock Photo: Kelvin Aitken / VWPics (c); WaterFrame (clb); Brandon Cole Marine Photography (cr). FLPA: Kelvin Aitken / Biosphoto (br). 4 Alamy Stock Photo: Kelvin Aitken / VWPics (cl, cr); Masa Ushioda / Stephen Frink Collection (crb). 4-5 Alamwy Stock Photo: Masa Ushioda / Stephen Frink Collection. 5 123RF. com: cbpix (tl). Alamy Stock Photo: Martin Strmiska (ca, cr). Getty Images: Auscape / Universal Images Group (clb, bl). 6-7 Alamy Stock Photo: Wild Wonders of Europe / Sá / Nature Picture Library. 6 Alamy Stock Photo: Brandon Cole Marine Photography (br); Doug Perrine (cl). 7 Dreamstime.com: Izanbar (ca). Getty Images: Wayne Lynch / All Canada Photos (c). 8 Dorling Kindersley: Natural History Museum, London (br). 10 Alamy Stock Photo: Barry Brown / Danita Delimont (clb). Getty Images: Banfi Franco / AGF / UIG / Universal Images Group (crb). 11 Alamy Stock Photo: Michael Patrick O'Neill (tl). Dorling Kindersley: Dr. Peter M. Forster (cra). SuperStock: Universal Images Group (crb). 12 Alamy Stock Photo: David Fleetham (cb, br); WaterFrame (bl, fbl). National Geographic Creative: Brian J. Skerry (tr). 13 Alamy Stock Photo: Kelvin Aitken / VWPics (tl, br); Marty Snyderman / Stephen Frink Collection (tc); blickwinkel / Hecker (cra); Masa Ushioda / Stephen Frink Collection (c); WaterFrame (bl). Getty Images: Jeff Rotman / Photolibrary (cr). 14-15 Alamy Stock Photo: Kelvin Aitken / VWPics. 14 Getty Images: Awashima Marine Park (cra). 15 Alamy Stock Photo: Kelvin Aitken / VWPics (tc); WaterFrame (b). FLPA: Kelvin Aitken / Biosphoto (cra). 16 FLPA: Kelvin Aitken / Biosphoto (bc). Getty Images: Paul Nicklen / National Geographic (bc). 16-17 Alamy Stock Photo: blickwinkel / Hecker. 17 Alamy Stock Photo: Kelvin Aitken / VWPics (bc, cb). 18-19 Alamy Stock Photo: Marty Snyderman / Stephen Frink Collection (t). Getty Images: Brian J. Skerry / National Geographic (b). 19 Alamy Stock Photo: Marty Snyderman / Stephen Frink Collection (t). 20-21 SuperStock: Universal Images Group (t). 21 Alamy Stock Photo: Kelvin Aitken / VWPics (cra); Jeff Rotman (cb). SuperStock: Universal Images Group (ca). 22 Alamy Stock Photo: Kelvin Aitken / VWPics (cla); Ben Horton / National Geographic Creative (cla); Norbert Probst / imageBROKER (clb). 22-23 Getty Images: Image Source. 23 Alamy Stock Photo: Charles Hood (cb); Michael Patrick O'Neill (bc). 24 Alamy Stock Photo: Natalia Pryanishnikova (bc). naturepl.com: Doug Perrine (cb). 24-25 Alamy Stock Photo: torstenvelden / RooM the Agency. 25 Getty Images: Jonathan Bird / Photolibrary (cb). 26 Alamy Stock Photo: ArteSub (bl);

WaterFrame (cb). 26-27 Alamy Stock Photo: Brandon Cole Marine Photography. 27 Dorling Kindersley: Jerry Young (bc). FLPA: Bruno Guenard / Biosphoto (c). Science Photo Library: Sandra J. Raredon, National Museum Of Natural History, Smithsonian Institution (cra). 28 Dorling Kindersley: Richard Davies of Oxford Scientific Films (bl, br). 29 Alamy Stock Photo: Fabrice Bettex (cra). Dorling Kindersley: Richard Davies of Oxford Scientific Films (bl); Suzanne Porter / Rough Guides (ca). 31 Getty Images: Doug Perrine / Photolibrary (br). 32 Alamy Stock Photo: Marevision / age fotostock (br, bc). 33 Alamy Stock Photo: Marevision / age fotostock (bl). naturepl.com: Doug Perrine (tr). 34-35 Getty Images: Brian J. Skerry / National Geographic. 35 Alamy Stock Photo: Image Source (ftr). Getty Images: Auscape / Universal Images Group (tr); Fleetham Dave / Perspectives (tl). 36 Alamy Stock Photo: Mark Conlin (br); Matt Heath (bl); Christian Zappel / imageBROKER (cr). 38 Alamy Stock Photo: Mark Conlin (cra). Getty Images: Jeff Rotman / Oxford Scientific (cla). naturepl.com: Alex Mustard / 2020Vision (ca). 38-39 Alamy Stock Photo: Reinhard Dirscherl (b). 39 Dorling Kindersley: Natural History Museum, London (c, bc). 40-41 Alamy Stock Photo: Dan Callister. 41 Alamy Stock Photo: Kelvin Aitken / VWPics (cr); Peter Mc Cabe (tr); David Fleetham (tl). National Geographic Creative: Bill Curtsinger (c). 42-43 Alamy Stock Photo: WaterFrame. 43 Alamy Stock Photo: digitalunderwater. com (cra). naturepl.com: Bruce Rasner / Rotman (crb). 45 Alamy Stock Photo: George Karbus Photography / Cultura RM (c); Matt Heath (ftl); WaterFrame (cr). Dorling Kindersley: Jerry Young (crb). 46 Getty Images: DEA Picture Library / De Agostini (bl). 47 Alamy Stock Photo: Andre Seale (cr). 48 Alamy Stock Photo: FLPA (bl). 49 Alamy Stock Photo: Ben Horton / National Geographic Creative (t); Carlos Villoch - MagicSea.com (ca); Rasmus Loeth Petersen (tc, cb); Jeff Rotman (b). Getty Images: Auscape / Universal Images Group (bc). 50-51 Dorling Kindersley: Merritt Cartographic / Ed Merritt (b). 52 Rob Allen: (tr, bl). 53 Rob Allen: (tl, tr, br). 54 The Trustees of the British Museum: Mike Row (tr). 55 Alamy Stock Photo: Steve Woods Photography / Cultura RM (cr). Getty Images: Steven Trainoff Ph.D. / Moment Select (tl). naturepl.com: Brandon Cole (bl). 56 Getty Images: Jim Abernethy / National Geographic (cl); Wayne Lynch / All Canada Photos (bl). 56-57 Alamy Stock Photo: WaterFrame. 57 Alamy Stock Photo: Reinhard Dirscherl (cra). naturepl.com: Bruce Rasner / Rotman (br). 60 Alamy Stock Photo: Brandon Cole Marine Photography (tl); Dan Callister (bl). 61 Dorling Kindersley: Jerry Young (tr). 62 Alamy Stock Photo: Reinhard Dirscherl (tl). 64 Alamy Stock Photo: WaterFrame (tl).

Cover images: Front: 123RF.com: Ten Theeralerttham crb; Alamy Stock Photo: Ben Horton / National Geographic Creative cla, WaterFrame cra; Dorling Kindersley: Natural History Museum, London tr, Jerry Young bc; SuperStock: Universal Images Group cr; Back:

Dorling Kindersley: Natural History Museum, London cla; Front Flap: Alamy Stock Photo: Brandon Cole Marine Photography cra/(hammerhead), Ben Horton / National Geographic Creative cra, Norbert Probst / imageBROKER cla, Masa Ushioda / Stephen Frink Collection cl; Dorling Kindersley: Dr. Peter M. Forster cr/ (inside), Natural History Museum, London cra/(inside), Natural History Museum, London crb; Getty Images: Wayne Lynch / All Canada Photos tr/ (inside); Back Endpapers: Alamy Stock Photo: Kelvin Aitken / VWPics 0 (frilled shark), blickwinkel / Hecker 0 (spiny dogfish), Brandon Cole Marine Photography 0 (hammerhead shark), Marty Snyderman / Stephen Frink Collection 0 (longnose sawshark), torstenvelden / RooM the Agency 0 (whale shark); Getty Images: Image Source 0 (great white shark), Brian J. Skerry / National Geographic 0 (prickly shark)

All other images © Dorling Kindersley

For further information see: www.dkimages.com

My Findout facts:

Cow and frilled sharks

Key features
- One dorsal fin
- Six or seven gill slits

One dorsal fin

Frilled shark

Bramble sharks

Key features
- Two dorsal fins
- Five gill slits
- Broad head
- Thorny skin
- No anal fin

Prickly shark

Sawsharks

Key features
- Two dorsal fins
- Five or six gill slits
- Saw-shaped nose with barbels
- No anal fin

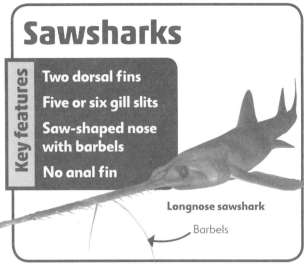

Longnose sawshark

Barbels

Angelsharks

Key features
- Two dorsal fins
- Five gill slits
- Flat-bodied
- No anal fin

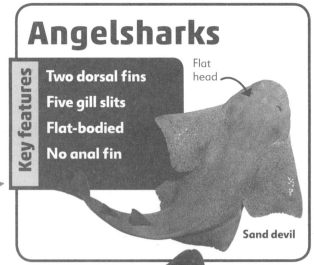

Flat head

Sand devil

Carpetsharks

Key features
- Two dorsal fins
- Five gill slits
- Mouth in front of eyes

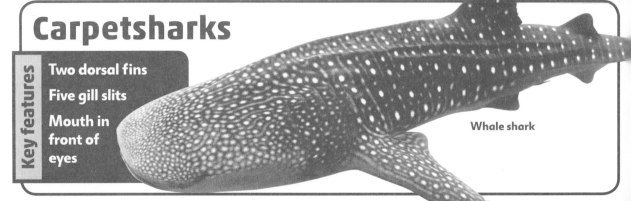

Whale shark